David Ortiz

Revised Edition

By Jeff Savage

Lerner Publications • Minneapolis

For Bailey Savage, my power-hitting son

Lerner Publications Company
A division of Lerner Publishing Group, Inc.
241 First Avenue North
Minneapolis, MN 55401 USA

For reading levels and more information, look up this title at www.lernerbooks.com.

Library of Congress Cataloging-in-Publication Data

Savage, Jeff, 1961–
    David Ortiz / by Jeff Savage. — Second revised edition.
        pages cm. — (Amazing athletes)
    Includes index.
    ISBN 978-1-4677-7584-7 (pbk. : alk. paper) — ISBN 978-1-4677-7586-1 (EB pdf)
    1. Ortiz, David, 1975– —Juvenile literature. 2. Baseball players—Dominican Republic—Biography—Juvenile literature. I. Title.
GV865.O78S28 2015
796.357092—dc23 [B]   2014032124

Manufactured in the United States of America
1 – BP – 12/31/14

TABLE OF CONTENTS

David Ortiz gets a hit in the first inning of Game 5 of the 2013 World Series.

"BORN FOR THIS"

David Ortiz of the Boston Red Sox walked to home plate in the first inning. He bent his knees and waited for the pitch. Crack! He sent the ball rocketing to the outfield. Dustin Pedroia ran home from second base. Boston had the lead, 1–0. David had come through again!

The Red Sox and the St. Louis Cardinals were playing Game 5 of the World Series. It was October 28, 2013. Each team had won two games so far. Game 5 was at Busch Stadium in St. Louis, Missouri. The Cardinals scored a run in the fourth inning. Then Boston scored two runs in the seventh. They held on to win the game, 3–1.

David *(left)* reaches to catch the ball for an out at first base.

David is one of the best batters in professional baseball.

David had been a huge part of Boston's success in the 2013 **regular season**. He had led the team in **batting average**, home runs, and **runs batted in (RBIs)**. He was even better in the World Series. After his **single** in the first inning, David's batting average against St. Louis was an incredible .750. He also had six RBIs and two home runs in the series. David wasn't surprised by his success. "I was born for this," he said after Game 5.

Game 6 was in Boston on October 30. The Cardinals pitched carefully to David. They tried to avoid throwing strikes. This made it harder for David to get a hit. But he was issued four **bases on balls**. He also scored two runs. The Red Sox won the game, 6–1. They were World Series champions!

David celebrates after scoring a run against the Cardinals in Game 6.

The Red Sox players stormed out of the **dugout** to celebrate on the field. The crowd cheered and snapped photos. Fireworks exploded in the night sky. David took the microphone and spoke to the fans. "This is for you, Boston," he said. "You guys deserve it."

David's .688 batting average was the second best in World Series history. He was named Most Valuable Player (MVP) of the series. David's nickname is Big Papi. In 2013, he came through for the Red Sox in a big way.

David holds up the 2013 World Series MVP trophy.

Young boys play baseball in the Dominican Republic. Many Dominican kids grow up hoping to become Major League Baseball (MLB) stars like David Ortiz.

GROWING UP HAPPY

David Américo Ortiz Arias was born November 18, 1975. His father's name is Américo. His mother's name is Angela Rosa Arias. David used the name Ortiz Arias until he was an adult.

David grew up in the Dominican Republic. This country is part of a large island southeast of Florida in the Caribbean Sea.

David's family lived in the country's capital, Santo Domingo.

David was a happy boy. He liked to laugh and joke around with his friends. He also liked to play sports. Baseball, basketball, and soccer were his favorites.

David grew up to be a big, strong kid. He was one of the best athletes in his neighborhood. David's best sport was baseball. He was a super hitter. He could smack the ball a long way.

Baseball is the most popular sport in the Dominican Republic. Children play the game on dirt fields. But many Dominican kids are too poor to buy bats and balls. So they use wooden sticks for bats and oranges for balls.

David was also a good basketball player. He was the best player on his team at Estudia Espallat High School. By this time, David was six feet four inches tall. He was so big and strong that most kids could not stop him from scoring baskets. David hoped he could become a pro athlete in one of his two favorite sports.

David is just one of many great MLB players from the Dominican Republic. Others include Francisco Liriano of the Pittsburgh Pirates, Albert Pujols of the Los Angeles Angels, and Melky Cabrera of the Toronto Blue Jays.

David practices at first base while playing for the Wisconsin Timber Rattlers.

MAKING THE BIG LEAGUES

David wasn't quite good enough to become a pro basketball player. But he had all the skills to be a great baseball hitter. He had quick hands. They helped him swing the bat fast enough to hit fast pitches. And he was very strong. This helped him to hit the ball a long way.

Scouts for Major League Baseball teams watched David play in high school. They saw him hit long home runs. The Seattle Mariners liked David's skills. In 1992, the Mariners offered David a **contract**. He signed on to play for a Mariners team in the **minor leagues**. David had just turned 17 years old. He would have to work his way up to the major leagues.

Early in 1994, David moved to the United States. He joined a Mariner minor-league team in Arizona. He enjoyed two great seasons. In 1996, the Mariners sent David to play for their minor-league team in Appleton, Wisconsin. Playing for the Wisconsin Timber Rattlers, he hit 34 **doubles**. He had a high batting average of .322 and smacked 18 home runs.

David and his wife, Tiffany, met when David was playing for the Timber Rattlers.

The Mariners traded David to the Minnesota Twins before the 1997 season. Around the same time, David dropped "Arias" from his name. He asked people to call him David Ortiz.

David had a huge year in 1997. He had a batting average over .300. In September, the Twins called him up to the major-league team. In his second game for the Twins, David smacked a double for his first major-league hit. A week later, he blasted his first home run. When the season ended, David had high hopes. He wanted to be the Twins' starting first baseman in 1998.

David *(right)* congratulates his teammate Jacque Jones after Jones hit a home run.

HARD TIMES

The 1998 season started out great for David. He began with a seven-game **hitting streak**. But then, he broke his wrist. He couldn't play for almost two months. But he played well when he returned to the Twins.

David's career with the Twins had many ups and downs.

David hoped to keep up his hot hitting in 1999. But he started out poorly in **spring training**. So the Twins sent him back to the minor leagues.

Playing for the Salt Lake Stingers, he cracked 30 home runs. He also led the league in RBIs. The Twins called David up to the major leagues. But he failed to get a hit in 20 at bats.

David returned to the Twins in 2000. But playing for the Twins wasn't always fun. They were a losing team. They lost 93 games and won only 69.

David had some bad times with the Twins, but he kept smiling. He kept his good sense of humor. He was always telling jokes and making his teammates laugh. David was a very popular player. His teammates liked him, and Twins fans liked him.

David *(left)* walks back to the dugout with his teammate Bobby Kielty after Kielty hit a home run.

But things kept going wrong in Minnesota. In 2001, David broke his wrist again. He missed a lot of games. When he got back, he struggled. David finished the year with a low .234 batting average.

But the biggest disaster hit David after the season. His mother was killed in a car accident. David was heartbroken. To remember her, he wears a big tattoo of her on his arm.

David proudly shows off the tattoo of his mother.

The Twins turned things around in 2002. David hit 20 home runs, and the Twins won 94 games. The team made it to the **playoffs** for the first time in years. Minnesota beat the Oakland A's in an exciting **American League Division Series (ALDS)**. Then they lost to the Los Angeles Angels. It had been a fun year. But David wasn't sure he would be back with the Twins in 2003.

After losing a playoff game, David sits quietly in the dugout. The 2002 playoffs would be the last games David played for the Twins.

David and his teammate Manny Ramirez *(left)* were the two best hitters in a powerful Red Sox lineup.

BOSTON HERO

After the 2002 season, the Twins didn't offer David a contract. He became a **free agent**. David joined the Boston Red Sox. He was thrilled to get a fresh start.

The Red Sox knew they had a star in David. Before the 2004 season, they signed him to a two-year contract for more than $12 million. David responded with a monster season. In 2004, his batting average was .301 and he hit 41 home runs. He also socked 47 doubles and added 139 RBIs. The Red Sox won 98 games and a spot in the playoffs.

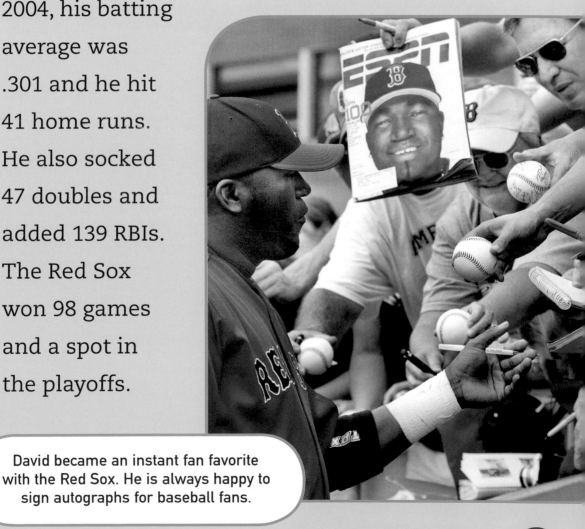

David became an instant fan favorite with the Red Sox. He is always happy to sign autographs for baseball fans.

David hit a game-winning home run to beat the Los Angeles Angels in the Division Series. But the Yankees pounded on the Red Sox in the first three games of the **American League Championship Series (ALCS)**. All seemed lost. No team had ever won a seven-game series after losing the first three games. But then David led Boston to wins in Game 4 and Game 5.

Suddenly, the Red Sox were on a roll. They needed two more wins to reach the World Series. Boston won with strong pitching in Game 6. Could they win Game 7?

In the first inning, David came to the plate with a runner on base. Bam! He crushed the ball for a home run! Boston cruised to a 10–3 win. The Red Sox were going to the World Series!

David and his team faced the mighty St. Louis Cardinals. St. Louis had plenty of strong players. But they were no match for

David *(left)* celebrates with his teammates after beating the Yankees in Game 7 of the ALCS.

Big Papi and his team. The Red Sox swept the series in four games. Boston had won the World Series! David and his teammates celebrated.

David celebrates with fans during a huge parade after the Red Sox World Series win in 2004.

So did the fans. More than one million people came out to watch the Red Sox victory parade a few days later. David loved every minute of it.

David had become one of MLB's best players. In 2005, he bashed 47 home runs and led the league with 148 runs batted in. He was even better in 2006. He finished first in the league with 54 home runs and 137 runs batted in.

In 2007, David had the fifth-best batting average and the fourth-most home runs in the American League. After knocking off the Los Angeles Angels and the Cleveland Indians in the playoffs, Boston faced the Colorado Rockies in the World Series. Once again, the Red Sox proved to be the better team in the biggest series of the year. Boston swept the Rockies for their second World Series victory in four years.

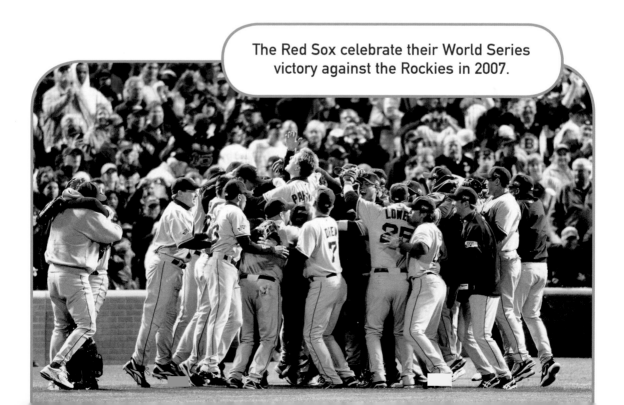

The Red Sox celebrate their World Series victory against the Rockies in 2007.

David sits in the dugout with his son, D'Angelo, in 2010.

David continued to mash the baseball during the next few seasons. Boston made the playoffs in 2008 and 2009. But they couldn't get back to the World Series. In 2010 and 2011, the Red Sox missed the playoffs completely.

David was frustrated by Boston's play. But he didn't let his team's problems affect his work off the field. He gives back to the community through the David Ortiz Children's Fund. The group helps provide money for sick children in the United States and the Dominican Republic. David also gives his time and money to hospitals in the Boston area. After the 2011 season, David was given a special honor. He was voted to receive the Roberto Clemente Award. Each year, this award is given to an MLB player who helps others off the field.

David stayed humble after winning the Roberto Clemente Award. He didn't help people to gain attention for himself. "You do as much as you can to help," David said. "We have a huge list of kids who are waiting to get their heart surgery."

Giving back to the community is important to David. Here he visits a patient at a Boston hospital.

In 2012, the Red Sox finished in last place in their **division**. They hadn't been to the playoffs since 2009. The team fired **manager** Bobby Valentine and hired John Farrell. That change paid off in 2013. David and Farrell led the Red Sox back to the World Series. For the third time in his career, David was a world champion.

David continues to inspire his fans. In 2014, he logged 35 home runs and racked up 104 RBIs. After 18 MLB seasons, the big slugger shows no signs of slowing down.

David gets a hit during a game in September 2014.

Selected Career Highlights

2014 Tallied 35 home runs and 104 RBIs for
        Boston

2013 Tallied 30 home runs and 103 RBIs for
        Boston
        Helped Boston win the World Series
        Named World Series MVP

2012 Tallied 23 home runs and 60 RBIs for Boston

2011 Tallied 29 home runs and 96 RBIs for Boston
        Named Roberto Clemente Award winner

2010 Tallied 32 home runs and 102 RBIs for
        Boston

2009 Tallied 28 home runs and 99 RBIs for Boston

2008 Tallied 23 home runs and 89 RBIs for Boston

2007 Tallied 35 home runs and 117 RBIs for Boston
        Helped Boston win the World Series

2006 Tallied 54 home runs and 137 RBIs for Boston

2005 Tallied 47 home runs and 148 RBIs for Boston

2004 Tallied 41 home runs and 139 RBIs for Boston
        Named ALCS MVP
        Helped Boston win the World Series

2003 Tallied 31 home runs and 101 RBIs for Boston

2002 Tallied 20 home runs and 75 RBIs for Minnesota

2001 Tallied 18 home runs and 48 RBIs for Minnesota

2000 Tallied 10 home runs and 63 RBIs for Minnesota

Glossary

American League Championship Series (ALCS): a series of games played to decide the winner of the American League. The team that wins four games in the series goes on to the World Series.

American League Division Series (ALDS): a series of games played after the regular season. The team that wins three games in the series goes on to the ALCS.

bases on balls: times when a batter is allowed to go to first base after not swinging at four pitches that were outside of the strike zone

batting average: a number that describes how often a baseball player makes a base hit

contract: a written agreement between a player and a team

division: a group of teams that play against one another. The MLB has six divisions.

doubles: two-base hits

dugout: the area next to the field where a baseball team sits

free agent: a player who is free to sign with any team

hitting streak: hitting safely in a number of games in a row

manager: the top coach on a baseball team

minor leagues: groups of teams in which players improve their skills and prepare to move to the majors

playoffs: games played to decide which team is the MLB champion

regular season: the main part of a baseball season. The best teams from the regular season go to the playoffs.

runs batted in (RBIs): the number of runners able to score on a batter's action, such as a hit or a walk

scouts: people who judge the skills of athletes

single: a one-base hit

spring training: a time from February through March when baseball teams train for the season

Further Reading & Websites

Braun, Eric. *Super Baseball Infographics*. Minneapolis: Lerner Publications, 2015.

Doeden, Matt. *The World Series: Baseball's Biggest Stage*. Minneapolis: Millbrook Press, 2014.

Fishman, Jon M. *Dustin Pedroia*. Minneapolis: Lerner Publications, 2015.

Kennedy, Mike, and Mark Stewart. *Long Ball: The Legend and Lore of the Home Run*. Minneapolis: Millbrook Press, 2006.

Boston Red Sox: The Official Site
http://boston.redsox.mlb.com/index.jsp?c_id=bos
The official website of the Boston Red Sox includes the team schedule and results, late-breaking news, biographies of past and present players and coaches, and much more.

Major League Baseball: The Official Site
http://mlb.mlb.com/home
Major League Baseball's official website provides fans with the latest scores and game schedules, as well as information on players, teams, and baseball history.

Sports Illustrated Kids
http://www.sikids.com
The *Sports Illustrated Kids* website covers all sports, including baseball.

LERNER

SOURCE

Expand learning beyond the printed book. Download free, complementary educational resources for this book from our website, www.lerneresource.com.

Index

Photo Acknowledgments

The images in this book are used with the permission of: © Jim Davis/ The Boston Globe via Getty Images, p. 4; © David Durochik/MLB Photos via Getty Images, pp. 5, 6; © Elsa/Getty Images, p. 7; © Ron Vesely/MLB Photos via Getty Images, p. 8; AP Photo/Wide World Photos, pp. 9, 21, 23; Wisconsin Timber Rattlers, p. 12; © Darren McCollester/Stringer/Getty Images, p. 14; AP Photo/Wide World Photos, p. 15; Minnesota Twins, p. 16; AP Photo/Wide World Photos, p. 17; © Chuck Rydlewski/Icon SMI, p. 18; AP Photo/Wide World Photos, p. 19; © Mike Segar/Reuters/CORBIS, p. 20; © Shawn Best/Reuters/ CORBIS, p. 24; © Jessica Rinaldi/Reuters/CORBIS, p. 25; © Michael Zagaris/ Getty Images, p. 26; © Darren McCollester/Getty Images for BCH, p. 27; © Patrick Smith/Getty Images, p. 28; © Mitchell Layton/Getty Images, p. 29.

Front cover: © Jim McIsaac/Getty Images.

Main body text set in Caecilia LT Std 55 Roman 16/28.
Typeface provided by Adobe Systems.